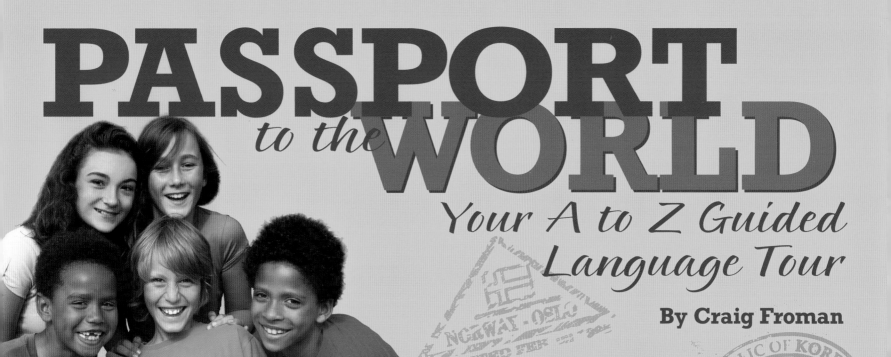

PASSPORT to the WORLD

Your A to Z Guided Language Tour

By Craig Froman

First Printing: October 2010
Fifth Printing: June 2021

Copyright © 2010 by Craig Froman and Master Books®. All rights reserved. No part of this book may be reproduced in any manner whatsoever without written permission of the publisher except in brief quotations in articles and reviews. For more information write: Master Books®, P.O. Box 726, Green Forest, AR 72638

PRINTED IN CHINA

Cover and Interior Design by Jennifer Bauer

ISBN 13: 978-0-89051-595-2
ISBN 13: 978-1-61458-333-2 (digital)

Library of Congress number: 2010910233

All Scripture references are New International Version unless otherwise noted.

Please visit our website for other great titles: www.masterbooks.com

Meet the author!

Find Craig Froman online here:

f **facebook.com/cmfroman**

Please consider requesting that a copy of this volume be purchased by your local library system.

Photo Credits: TL = top left, BL = bottom left, TR = top right, BR = bottom right
All photos are from Shutterstock unless otherwise noted.
Bank of Canada: 18B
Bryan Miller: 6
IStock.com: 8TL, 11TL, 17BR, 18TR, 22TR, 41BR, 45TL, 47BR, 51BR, 54TR, 55BL, 57BR, 58BR, 59BR
NASA: 17TL
Saffron Blaze, via http://www.mackenzie.co: 19LT
Wikipedia: 19BR, 19LM, 29TL, 31BR, 39TL, 46B, 58BR
All data for the country fast facts has been referenced from the Central Intelligence Agency (cia.gov) and updated 2017.

Master Books®
A Division of New Leaf Publishing Group
www.masterbooks.com

Welcome to the start of an incredible language journey around the world! Your book is set up by various world languages, organized A to Z. You will cross countries and continents, all the while in the comfort of your own living room, car, or backyard tent!

1 **Language:** Here you will find the specific language focus of the country you are visiting. This may be the primary language of the country, or it may be a special language that only a few people speak in the world!

2 **Country:** This is the name of the specific nation you are visiting. Most of the facts listed will relate to the country, not necessarily the language spoken. Learn insights about cultural and traditional customs, as well as how to fit in when you stay.

3 **Country fast facts:** Here you can quickly find out details about the country, including its flag, size in square miles, how many people live there, how long the average person lives, how many can read and write based on those age 15 and over, Internet information, and what kind of money the people use. Find the highlighted country and its capital city, as well as where it is in relation to neighboring countries or oceans.

KOREAN

1

A language spoken in

SOUTH KOREA

2

11

COUNTRY FAST FACTS

3

NORTH KOREA

SEA OF JAPAN (EAST SEA)

★ Seoul

YELLOW SEA

Square Miles: 38,502

Population: 51,181,299

Life Expectancy: 82 years

Literacy: 97.9%

Internet Users: 44,153,000

Internet Code: .kr

Money Unit: South Korean won

SPEAKING KOREAN

5

Hello: Annyong (an nyong)
Goodbye: Annyong-hi kasipsio (an nyong sheep see oh)
Thank you: Kamsahamnida (come sam needah)
Peace: Phyongh'wa (pea young wah)

6

4

Annyong

Hello from South Korea! Here there are over 51,000,000 people, most of whom speak Korean. Look at the map and you will see our capital city of Seoul. Its name simply means "the capital" in Korean! Though there are many Protestants, Roman Catholics, and Buddhists here, almost 50 percent of our country does not claim any religion. Kamsahamnida for your visit! Find phyongh'wa today.

Annyong-hi kashipshio.

28

4 **Greeting from a friend:** Read a welcome from a friend to learn more about the country, as well as to see how the words from the language are used.

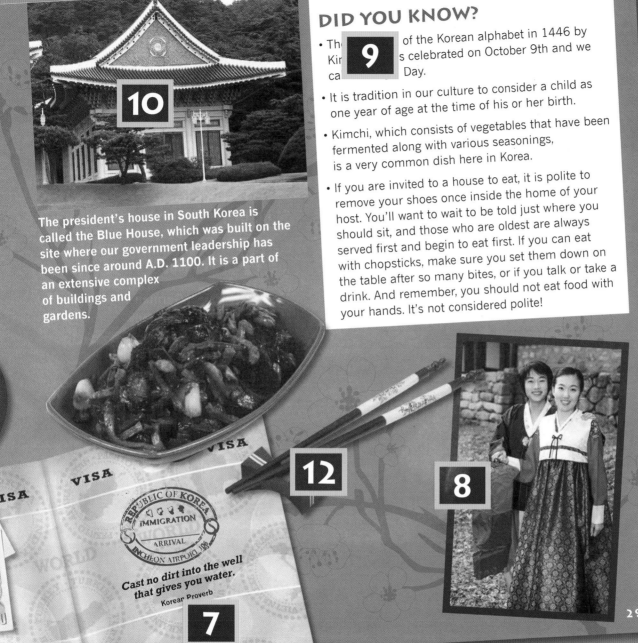

10

The president's house in South Korea is called the Blue House, which was built on the site where our government leadership has been since around A.D. 1100. It is a part of an extensive complex of buildings and gardens.

DID YOU KNOW?

9

- The ___ of the Korean alphabet in 1446 by Kin____ ___s celebrated on October 9th and we ca___ ___ Day.

- It is tradition in our culture to consider a child as one year of age at the time of his or her birth.

- Kimchi, which consists of vegetables that have been fermented along with various seasonings, is a very common dish here in Korea.

- If you are invited to a house to eat, it is polite to remove your shoes once inside the home of your host. You'll want to wait to be told just where you should sit, and those who are oldest are always served first and begin to eat first. If you can eat with chopsticks, make sure you set them down on the table after so many bites, or if you talk or take a drink. And remember, you should not eat food with your hands. It's not considered polite!

VISA
VISA
VISA

REPUBLIC OF KOREA
IMMIGRATION
ARRIVAL
INCHEON AIRPORT

Cast no dirt into the well that gives you water.
Korean Proverb

7

12

8

29

7 **Country proverb:** Read a common saying that comes from that nation.

8 **Traditional picture:** This picture most often shows someone dressed in one of the traditional or customary outfits of the nation or a specific people group in the nation.

9 **Did you know?:** Here you will learn interesting facts about each country or language.

10 **Geographic picture:** This picture shows a little something interesting about the country, its cities, mountains, lakes, and more.

11 **Current picture:** This picture shows what the people look like in their everyday clothing.

12 **Images:** See items that are found in the specific country you're visiting and mentioned in the Did You Know? section.

5 **Speaking the language:** Learn how to say hello, goodbye, thank you, and peace in a specific language used in that country.

6 **Money:** See images of the country's currency.

A MAP OF YOUR LANGUAGE JOURNEY

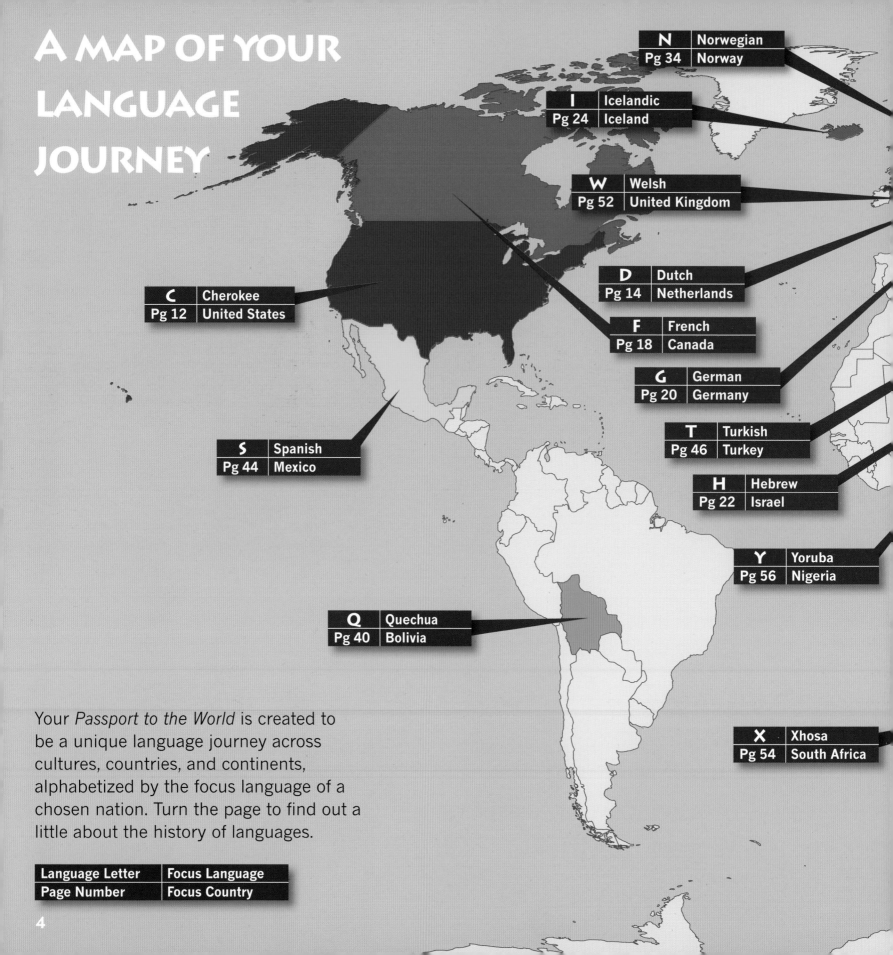

N	Norwegian
Pg 34	Norway

I	Icelandic
Pg 24	Iceland

W	Welsh
Pg 52	United Kingdom

D	Dutch
Pg 14	Netherlands

C	Cherokee
Pg 12	United States

F	French
Pg 18	Canada

G	German
Pg 20	Germany

S	Spanish
Pg 44	Mexico

T	Turkish
Pg 46	Turkey

H	Hebrew
Pg 22	Israel

Y	Yoruba
Pg 56	Nigeria

Q	Quechua
Pg 40	Bolivia

X	Xhosa
Pg 54	South Africa

Your *Passport to the World* is created to be a unique language journey across cultures, countries, and continents, alphabetized by the focus language of a chosen nation. Turn the page to find out a little about the history of languages.

Language Letter	Focus Language
Page Number	Focus Country

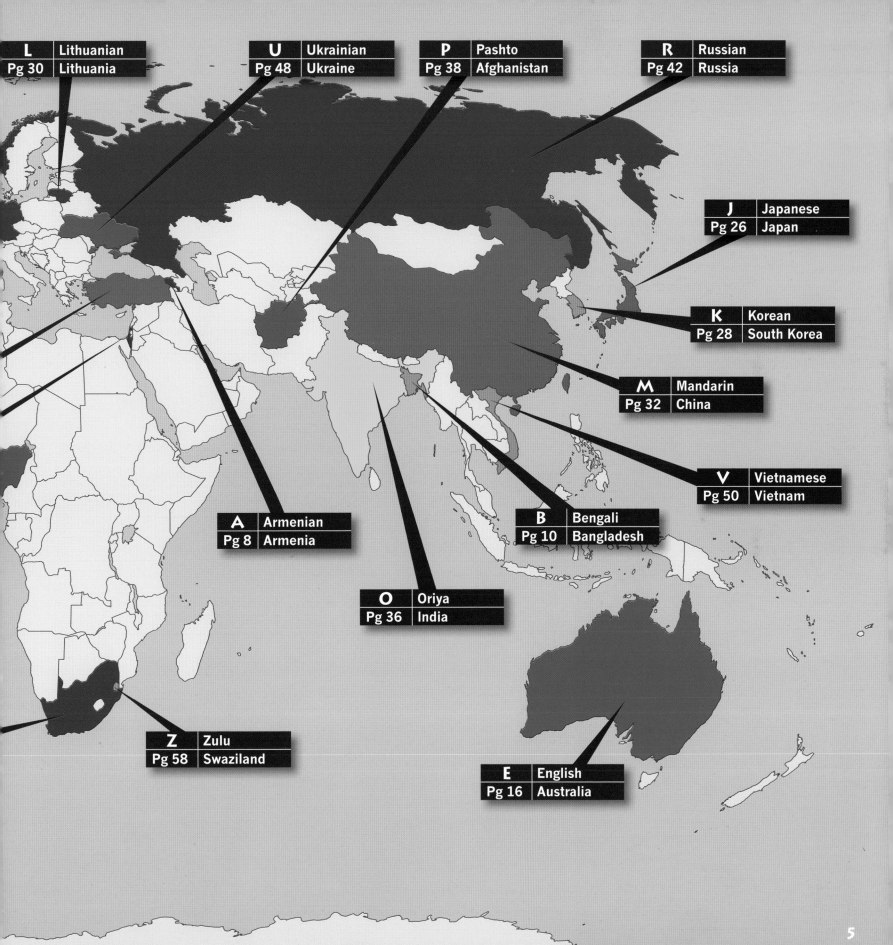

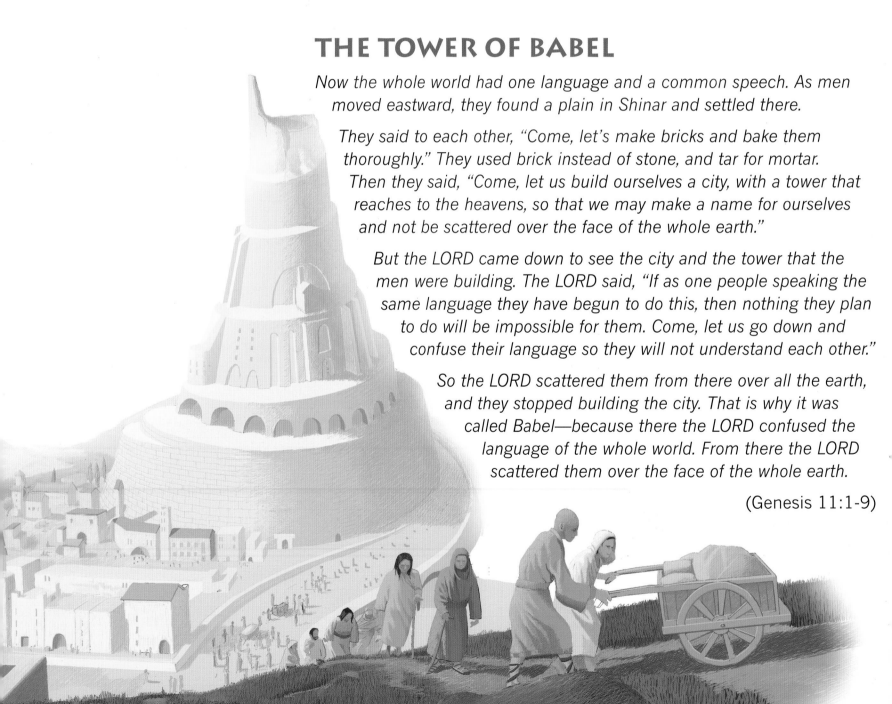

WHERE OUR STORY BEGINS...

Just over 4,000 years ago, most people lived on a plain in Shinar, which would have been located in what is now called the Middle East. Though God wanted them to fill the earth (Genesis 9:1), they were determined to stay and build a tower to show how great they were. Here is the account of where it all started.

THE TOWER OF BABEL

Now the whole world had one language and a common speech. As men moved eastward, they found a plain in Shinar and settled there.

They said to each other, "Come, let's make bricks and bake them thoroughly." They used brick instead of stone, and tar for mortar. Then they said, "Come, let us build ourselves a city, with a tower that reaches to the heavens, so that we may make a name for ourselves and not be scattered over the face of the whole earth."

But the LORD came down to see the city and the tower that the men were building. The LORD said, "If as one people speaking the same language they have begun to do this, then nothing they plan to do will be impossible for them. Come, let us go down and confuse their language so they will not understand each other."

So the LORD scattered them from there over all the earth, and they stopped building the city. That is why it was called Babel—because there the LORD confused the language of the whole world. From there the LORD scattered them over the face of the whole earth.

(Genesis 11:1-9)

LANGUAGE FAMILIES

After their languages were changed, all these people (listed in Genesis Chapter 10) began to move off with those they could best communicate with (their families). These language families have now spread throughout the world, and though languages have continued to change, we tend to relate best to those we share a common speech with.

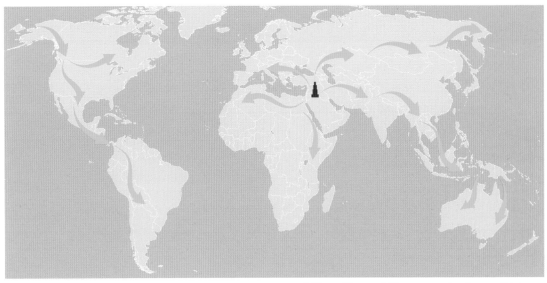

Migration of the people from Shinar

From those who came from the Tower of Babel between 6,800 and 6,900 languages have arisen, over 2,200 of which have a written form. Also, many languages are spoken by people outside the country that is known for it, and many speak another language as a secondary one.

FILLING THE EARTH

Language groups spread out across the lands, now covering the world, even a few researchers in Antarctica! The seven areas we call continents are from largest in size to smallest: Asia, Africa, North America, South America, Antarctica, Europe, and Australia.

WHERE OUR STORY WILL END

One day, God will gather His people together from every nation and language group:

> "After this I looked and there before me was a great multitude that no one could count, from every nation, tribe, people and language, standing before the throne and in front of the Lamb. They were wearing white robes and were holding palm branches in their hands."

(Revelation 7:9)

LET'S GO!

Now, let's find out where 26 distinct languages from A to Z are spoken! Grab your passport and let's get ready, steady, and go!

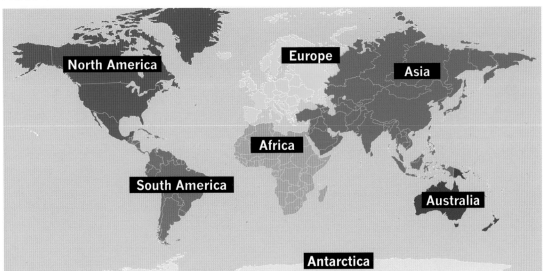

The Seven Continents

ARMENIAN

A language spoken in

ARMENIA

COUNTRY FAST FACTS

GEORGIA   GEORGIA

AZERBAIJAN

Yerevan ★

TURKEY

AZERBAIJAN

IRAN

Square Miles: 11,483

Population:	3,045,191
Life Expectancy:	75 years
Literacy:	99.7%
Internet Users:	1,891,775
Internet Code:	.am
Money Unit:	Drams

SPEAKING ARMENIAN

Hello: Parev (paw rev)

Goodbye: Tsedesutyun (se dess you toon)

Thank you: Shnorhagallem (snore hey gall em)

Peace: Khanaghutyun (can agg yoot yoon)

Parev!

That is how we say "hello" here in Armenia. Shnorhagallem for coming by! Armenian is spoken by approximately six million people around the world. Nearly half of those live in my country, which has a population of 3,045,191. Look closely at the map of my country and you will see Yerevan. This is our capital city, and is one of the oldest cities in the world. We were the first nation to adopt Christianity, way back in the 4th century! Our major religions are Armenian Apostolic, Christian, and Yezidi. Khanaghutyun to you.

Tsedesutyun, friend!!!

The region of Ararat is the highest mountain range in the country. This is the area where Noah's ark came to rest after the Flood.

As mills require two stones, so friendship requires two heads.
Armenian Proverb

DID YOU KNOW?

- If you need to find a place that serves sandwiches or coffee, look for a chasharan. It's what you might say is a typical café, Armenian style. And try not to yawn while talking to the people who are there. It's considered very rude!

- If you like fruit, the apricots grown here are considered the best tasting in the world! And if you fancy some dessert, the bakeries, called entrikners, sell the usual cakes and cookies, as well as traditional walnut and honey treats and Christmas pastries called gata.

- The Armenian language has borrowed many words from Greek, Persian, Russian, and Turkish.

- Since about A.D. 400 we have had our own distinct language and alphabet.

- They have found ancient cuneiform writings here that use pictures to communicate, rather than letters. This shows just how long ago people have lived here!

BENGALI

A language spoken in

BANGLADESH

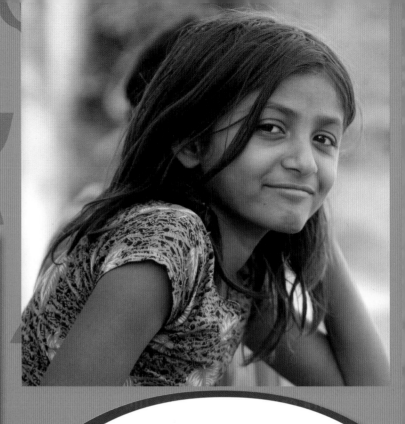

COUNTRY FAST FACTS

NEPAL

INDIA

Dhaka ★

BAY OF BENGAL

BURMA

Square Miles: 55,597

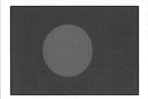

Population: 157,826,578

Life Expectancy: 73 years

Literacy: 72.8%

Internet Users: 28,499,324

Internet Code: .bd

Money Unit: Taka

SPEAKING BENGALI

Hello: Nomoskar (no mo scar)
Goodbye: Accha (ah cha)
Thank you: Dhanyabad (doon yaw bawd)
Peace: Shanti (shawn tee)

Nomoskar!

Saying hello from Bangladesh! I speak Bengali, along with over 200 million other people from around the world, about half of whom live here in my country. If you look in the center of the map you can see our capital city, Dhaka. Here in our country we have 157,826,578 people, and the major religions are Muslim, Hindu, and a few others. We are known for our wonderful teas that we ship around the world. Dhanyabad for stopping by! Shanti to you and your family.

Accha, friend!!!

Our country, known officially as the Republic of Bangladesh, became recognized as a nation in 1971. The word "Bengali" in English relates to all of us who speak the language, as well as to the language itself.

DID YOU KNOW?

- All of our Bengali literature was in rhymed verse if written prior to the 19th century.

- Bangladesh has a coastal mangrove forest, which is part of the Sundarbans National Park, and is one of the largest such forests in the world.

- The Nobel Peace Prize was given to the Grameen Bank in Bangladesh for its help in providing assistance to many of the poor in the country, especially many of our impoverished women.

- The people here eat a lot of fish and rice, and sometimes because of rice farming, weather, and other natural conditions, as much as 80 percent of our land can be covered in water. Also, we use a lot of spices to flavor our food, but some favorites include coriander, cumin, garlic, ginger, and turmeric.

VISA

VISA

APPROVED
BANGLADESH

A handful of love is better than an oven full of bread.
Bengali Proverb

CHEROKEE

A language spoken in the

UNITED STATES OF AMERICA

COUNTRY FAST FACTS

CANADA

Washington D.C.★

MEXICO   CUBA

Square Miles: 3,794,100

Population:
326,625,791

Life Expectancy:
80 years

Literacy:
99%

Internet Users:
246,809,221

Internet Code:
.us

Money Unit:
Dollar

SPEAKING CHEROKEE

Hello: Ohseeyo (oh see yo)

Goodbye: Donadagovi
(doe naw doe go vee)

Thank you: Wado (waw doe)

Peace: Dohiyi (doe hee yee)

Ohseeyo!

Saying hello in Cherokee! Most of the 326,625,791 people in the United States speak English, and Cherokee is spoken by just over 20,000 people, mostly in Oklahoma and North Carolina. Our capital city is Washington, DC, on the far eastern shore of our country. The word Cherokee comes from the word Muskogee, and means "those who speak another language." There are many religions in the United States, including Protestants, Roman Catholics, Mormons, Jewish, Buddhist, Muslim, and others. Wado for being here! May you have dohiyi.

Donadagovi, friend!!!

There are approximately 8.5 million takeoffs per year at American airports, which is almost half of the flights around the world.

Always remember that a smile is something sacred, to be shared.
Cherokee Proverb

VISA
VISA
USA IMMIGRATION OFFICER 6079

DID YOU KNOW?

- The postal service here in the United States moves over 40 percent of the world's mail on any given day.

- The majority of people in the United States speak English as their primary language, though people from all over the world have come to live here and there is no official language.

- Cherokee is considered an endangered language, though many are trying to ensure that the language and culture survive, including the art form of basket making.

- There are more personal computers in the United States than in the next four biggest purchasers combined: Japan, China, Germany and the United Kingdom.

- We really like our popcorn here, eating over 17 billion quarts of popped popcorn every year. That averages to over 65 quarts per person! We also like our pizza, eating on average about 100 acres of pizza every day or 350 slices every second!

DUTCH

A language spoken in the

NETHERLANDS

COUNTRY FAST FACTS

NORTH SEA

U.K.

★ Amsterdam

GERMANY

FRANCE

BELGIUM

LUX.

Square Miles: 16,039

Population:	17,084,719
Life Expectancy:	81 years
Literacy:	99%
Internet Users:	15,385,203
Internet Code:	.nl
Money Unit:	Euros

SPEAKING DUTCH

Hello: Dag or goededag (dawg or gude dawg)

Goodbye: Tot ziens (tote scenes)

Thank you: Dank u (dawn koo)

Peace: Vrede (vrey day)

Daag!

Hello from the Netherlands! If you look at the map you'll find that beautiful Amsterdam is our capital city. I speak Dutch, a language spoken by about 23 million people around the world. Around 12 million of those people live here in the Netherlands. Our total population is 17,084,719 people, with a mix of religious faiths including Roman Catholic, Dutch Reformed, Calvinist, Muslim, and a few others. Dank u for being my friend! Vrede to you.

Tot ziens, friend!!!

14

The 800 miles of dikes built in the Netherlands help hold back waters from the sea that would at times cover 40 percent of our land. One-fourth of our country is actually below sea level.

DID YOU KNOW?

- People here love riding bikes, and you'll find more than twice as many bikes as cars in the country.

- Dutch, sometimes known as Flemish or Vlaams, is spoken by most people here, as well as by many people living in Belgium, the northern region of France, the island of Aruba, and by over half of the people in Suriname.

- The Netherlands is often associated with our beautiful tulips, found here by the millions, and the old style wooden shoes, or clogs, which were worn to protect workers in factories and mines.

- Many wonderful artists have come from the Netherlands including Rembrandt, Jan Steen, Vincent van Gogh, and Jan Vermeer, as well as inventions that include the microscope, pendulum clock, telescope, and mercury thermometer.

- Many people here enjoying eating raw herring with onions sprinkled over it.

VISA

NETHERLANDS REPUBLIC

WORLD

ACCEPTED

A friend at one's back is a safe bridge.
Dutch Proverb

ENGLISH

A language spoken in AUSTRALIA

COUNTRY FAST FACTS

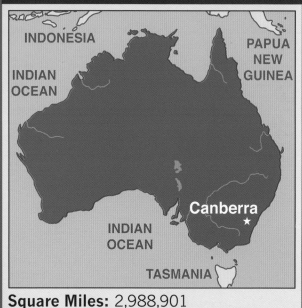

INDONESIA

INDIAN OCEAN

PAPUA NEW GUINEA

Canberra

INDIAN OCEAN

TASMANIA

Square Miles: 2,988,901

Population:
23,232,413

Life Expectancy:
82 years

Literacy:
99%

Internet Users:
20,288,409

Internet Code:
.au

Money Unit:
Australian Dollars

SPEAKING ENGLISH

Hello: Hello or hullo (he low or ha low)
Goodbye: Goodbye (good buy)
Thank you: Thank you (thanck yoo)
Peace: Peace (peece)

Hello!

Thank you for coming here to see me! I live in Australia, which just happens to be the only country that is also a continent. Also, it's the only continent that doesn't have an active volcano! There are just over 340 million English speakers worldwide, and as many as one billion who can speak it as a second language! It is the official language of over 50 countries, one of which is mine. Here we have just over 23,000,000 people, who follow various religious beliefs including Catholic, Anglican, other Christian, Buddhist, Muslim, and others. If you look at the map, on the southeast you will find Canberra, our capital city. May you have peace this day.

Goodbye, friend!!!

Australia is very large. On the Nullarbor Plain you will find 100,000 square miles of land without a single tree, as seen in this satellite photo.

IMMIGRATION
ARRIVED
SYDNEY AIRPORT
4251
AUSTRALIA

You can't judge a book by its cover.
English Proverb

DID YOU KNOW?

- More unique reptile species can be found in Australia than in all other countries combined.

- The English language originally came from the Germanic tribes of Angles, Jutes, and Saxons who came to the British Isles around A.D. 450. The Old Norse language of the 8th and 9th centuries that was used by the Vikings truly affected the roots of English too.

- There are countries that use English as a first or second language on all five continents, which amounts to nearly half of the population of the world.

- Though English has more words than any other language, most people who speak English use only about one percent of them!

- Quite a few inventions came from Australia including aspirin, the black-box flight recorder, long-wearing contact lenses, note pads, and penicillin.

- The didgeridoo or didge is a unique wind instrument to our country, and is thought to be over a thousand years old based on cave paintings.

FRENCH

A language spoken in

CANADA

COUNTRY FAST FACTS

GREENLAND

Ottawa ★

UNITED STATES OF AMERICA

Square Miles: 3,855,102

Population: 35,623,680

Life Expectancy: 82 years

Literacy: 99%

Internet Users: 31,770,034

Internet Code: .ca

Money Unit: Canadian dollars

SPEAKING FRENCH

Hello: Bonjour (bone ju)
Goodbye: Au revoir (oh ev wah)
Thank you: Merci (mare see)
Peace: Paix (pay)

Bonjour!

That's how I say hello in Canada! I live in our capital city of Ottawa. In our country you will find around 8 million people who speak French, while some 220 million speak it around the world, with some of those speaking it as their second language. Over 35 million people live in Canada. Of these, there are those who are Catholic, Protestant, Muslim, Hindu, Sikh, Buddhist, Jewish, and non-religious citizens. Merci beaucoup for coming so far! Hope you are filled with paix.

Au revoir, friend!!!

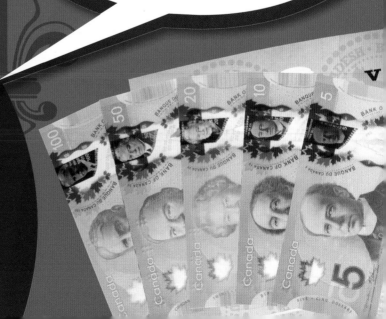

18

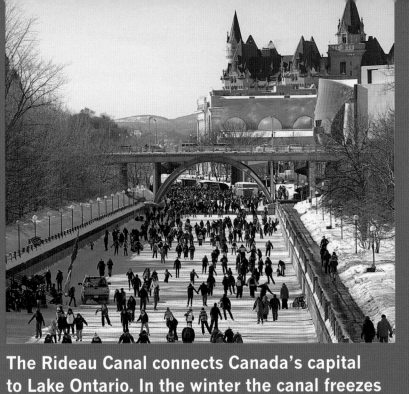

The Rideau Canal connects Canada's capital to Lake Ontario. In the winter the canal freezes over and becomes the longest skateway in the world at 4.8 miles.

DID YOU KNOW?

- French is spoken as a first or second language in over 50 countries, including Algeria, Haiti, Morocco, and Switzerland.

- Basketball was invented by a Canadian physical education instructor. Dr. James Naismith came up with the game in 1891 while teaching at Springfield College in Springfield, Massachusetts.

- With over 40 percent of Canadians either the first or second generation of their family to live in the country, nearly 20 percent of the population was born in another country and moved here.

- Many Canadians love eating poutine, which was originally simply a dish of French fries covered in cheese curds and gravy. Also, we produce over 70 percent of the world's supply of maple syrup, making such things as syrup on a stick, maple leaf cream cookies, and maple toffee.

VISA

Immigration Canada 345
345
WORLD
345
TORONTO
345

Patience is a tree whose root is bitter, but its fruit is very sweet.
Canadian Proverb

GERMAN
A language spoken in
GERMANY

COUNTRY FAST FACTS

Square Miles: 137,846

Population:	80,594,017
Life Expectancy:	81 years
Literacy:	99%
Internet Users:	72,365,643
Internet Code:	.de
Money Unit:	Euros

SPEAKING GERMAN

Hello: Guten tag (goo ten tawk)

Goodbye: Auf wiedersehen (owf veda sayin)

Thank you: Danke (dawn ka)

Peace: Frieden (free den)

Guten tag!

Saying hello from Germany where just over 80,594,017 people live! Approximately 80,000,000 people speak German here, as well as in Austria. Around one-third of our population is Protestant, one-third is Roman Catholic, and the other people include other faiths and those with no religious beliefs. Near the northeastern side of our country you find Berlin, our capital. Danke for your visit! Frieden to you.

Auf wiedersehen, friend!!!

The tallest church in the world is the Ulm Cathedral, which stands 530 feet high.

Better an honest enemy than a false friend.
German Proverb

DID YOU KNOW?

- The first Bible ever printed was printed in Germany. In 1456, Johannes Gutenberg printed the Bible in Mainz, and this new printing press would open the doors of the Scripture to the common people. Prior to this, only a few people in Church leadership had access to God's Word.

- Nearly one quarter of Americans have at least some German heritage.

- The Zooligischer Garten in Berlin is the world's largest zoo, with around 1,500 animal species and nearly 14,000 creatures.

- Many classical music composers were German, including Bach, Beethoven, Brahms, Mendelssohn, Schumann, and Wagner.

- Several countries outside of Germany have German as an official language (such as Austria, Belgium, and Italy), as a local official language (such as areas of Denmark and Poland), or where it is simply spoken by a certain group of locals (such as Namibia and various Amish communities in America).

- Baked pretzels have been a part of German heritage since at least the 12th century. They were often hidden on the morning of Easter, much like some people hide eggs.

HEBREW
A language spoken in
ISRAEL

COUNTRY FAST FACTS

Population:	8,299,706
Life Expectancy:	82 years
Literacy:	97.8%
Internet Users:	6,521,539
Internet Code:	.il
Money Unit:	New Israeli Shekels

Square Miles: 8,019

Map labels: LEBANON, SYRIA, MEDITERRANEAN SEA, WEST BANK, Jerusalem, GAZA STRIP, JORDAN, EGYPT

SPEAKING HEBREW

Hello: Shalom (shaw lome)
Goodbye: Lehitrahott (leh hee trah oht)
Thank you: Toda (toe da)
Peace: Shalom (shaw lome)

Shalom!

Hello from Israel! There are about 8,300,000 people in Israel, 75 percent of whom are Jewish, with five million speaking Hebrew here. There are also Muslims, Arab Christians, Christians, Druze, and others who live here, too. Our capital city is Jerusalem, one of the oldest cities in the world! Toda for your good visit! May you and your family find shalom.

Lehitrahott, friend!!!

The lowest dry land on earth is found here at the Dead Sea, also called the Salt Sea because there is so much salt you can float. It is around 1,315 feet below sea level.

DID YOU KNOW?

- Hebrew is the original language of the Old Testament, with Moses recording the first five books of the Bible (called the Torah) around 3,300 years ago, mentioning pomegranates even then.

- The money here in Israel actually has Braille printed into it so the blind can identify the amount of the bills.

- There are more museums per person in Israel than in any other country in the world, so you can be sure to find something of interest!

- The language of the Jewish people began to fade as a spoken language soon after they were captured around 586 B.C. by the Babylonians. Aramaic became the main language of my people at that time, though Hebrew was still used in writing and religion. Hebrew again became a living language through the influence of Eliezer Ben-Yehuda, who moved from Russia to Palestine in 1881.

- The nine branch Hanukkah menorah has been rooting in Jewish tradition for over 2,000 years.

VISA
VISA
VISA
ISRAEL
IMMIGRATION OFFICER
Customs -Jerusalem

Promise little and do much.
Hebrew Proverb

ICELANDIC

A language spoken in

ICELAND

COUNTRY FAST FACTS

GREENLAND

Reykjavik

NORTH ATLANTIC OCEAN

ARTIC CIRCLE

Square Miles: 39,768

Population:
339,747

Life Expectancy:
83 years

Literacy:
99%

Internet Users:
329,967

Internet Code:
.is

Money Unit:
Icelandic Kronur

SPEAKING ICELANDIC

Hello: Góðan dag (go den dock)
Goodbye: Bless (ble sh)
Thank you: Takk (taw ck)
Peace: Friður (free door)

Góðan dag!

That's my way to say hello here in Iceland! Icelandic is spoken by most of the 339,747 people in my country. See if you can find our capital city, Reykjavik, on the map. It's on the coast as are most of our main cities. Most people here attend the Lutheran Church of Iceland, but there are also Roman Catholics, other Christian denominations, and a few other religions. Takk for coming by today! Be at Friður.

Bless, friend!!!

24

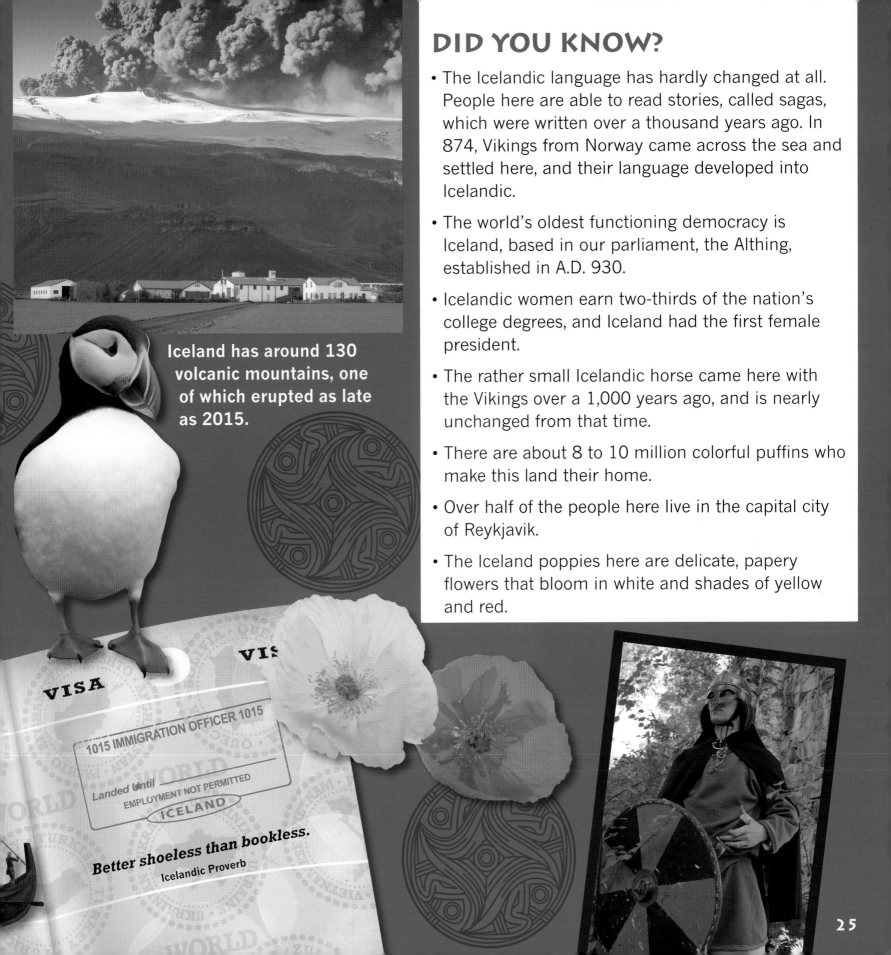

Iceland has around 130 volcanic mountains, one of which erupted as late as 2015.

DID YOU KNOW?

- The Icelandic language has hardly changed at all. People here are able to read stories, called sagas, which were written over a thousand years ago. In 874, Vikings from Norway came across the sea and settled here, and their language developed into Icelandic.

- The world's oldest functioning democracy is Iceland, based in our parliament, the Althing, established in A.D. 930.

- Icelandic women earn two-thirds of the nation's college degrees, and Iceland had the first female president.

- The rather small Icelandic horse came here with the Vikings over a 1,000 years ago, and is nearly unchanged from that time.

- There are about 8 to 10 million colorful puffins who make this land their home.

- Over half of the people here live in the capital city of Reykjavik.

- The Iceland poppies here are delicate, papery flowers that bloom in white and shades of yellow and red.

VISA

VISA

1015 IMMIGRATION OFFICER 1015

Landed until

EMPLOYMENT NOT PERMITTED

ICELAND

Better shoeless than bookless.
Icelandic Proverb

JAPANESE

A language spoken in

JAPAN

COUNTRY FAST FACTS

RUSSIA

CHINA

NORTH KOREA

Tokyo ★

SOUTH KOREA

Square Miles: 145,913

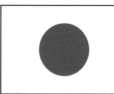

Population:	126,451,398
Life Expectancy:	85 years
Literacy:	99%
Internet Users:	116,565,962
Internet Code:	.jp
Money Unit:	Yen

SPEAKING JAPANESE

Hello: Konnichiwa (ko nee chee wah)
Goodbye: Sayonara (sigh oh nara)
Thank you: Arigatou (a ree gat oh)
Peace: Heiwa (hi wah)

Konnichiwa!

Just saying hello from Japan! Our capital city is Tokyo. Here in Japan about 122,000,000 people speak Japanese and we have just under 127,000,000 people here. Our major religions are Shinto and Buddhist, though there are other religions present including a small number of Christians. Arigatou for stopping to see me! May you have heiwa today.

Sayonara, friend!!!

Japan is a land of earthquakes and volcanoes and we build our skyscrapers to be able to sway when the earth shakes. This allows for the metal and cement to ride out the quakes with little or no damage. Above is our Rainbow Bridge that crosses Tokyo Bay.

DID YOU KNOW?

- They have discovered ancient pyramid structures in the ocean off our coast. In 1986, a diver near the island of Yonaguni Jima came across some strange stones under the sea. They appeared to be step-like forms with terraces and ramps. One of the largest pyramid buildings is 600 feet wide and 90 feet high with what looks like a road surrounding it.

- They say that three-fourths of the kids here in Japan read comic books.

- Farms here are fairly small, with an average of 3 acres, while farms in the United States have an average of 467 acres of land. Rice is one of the foods that are grown extensively across Japan.

- If you want to get around in Tokyo, you might want to take a bike if the trip is under an hour. It will be faster than a car!

Adversity is the foundation of virtue.
Japanese Proverb

KOREAN

A language spoken in

SOUTH KOREA

COUNTRY FAST FACTS

NORTH KOREA

SEA OF JAPAN (EAST SEA)

★ Seoul

YELLOW SEA

Square Miles: 38,502

Population: 51,181,299

Life Expectancy: 82 years

Literacy: 97.9%

Internet Users: 44,153,000

Internet Code: .kr

Money Unit: South Korean won

SPEAKING KOREAN

Hello: Annyeong (an nyoung)

Goodbye: Annyong-hi kashipshio (an nyoung cah sheep shoe)

Thank you: Kamsahamnida (come sam needah)

Peace: Phyongh'wa (pea young wah)

Annyeong!

Hello from South Korea! Here there are over 51,000,000 people, most of whom speak Korean. Look at the map and you will see our capital city of Seoul. Its name simply means "the capital" in Korean! Though there are many Protestants, Roman Catholics, and Buddhists here, almost 50 percent of our country does not claim any religion. Kamsahamnida for your visit! Find phyongh'wa today.

Annyong-hi kashipshio.

The president's house in South Korea is called the Blue House, which was built on the site where our government leadership has been since around A.D. 1100. It is a part of an extensive complex of buildings and gardens.

Cast no dirt into the well that gives you water.
Korean Proverb

DID YOU KNOW?

- The founding of the Korean alphabet in 1446 by King Sejong is celebrated on October 9th and we call it Hangul Day.

- It is tradition in our culture to consider a child as one year of age at the time of his or her birth.

- Kimchi, which consists of vegetables that have been fermented along with various seasonings, is a very common dish here in Korea.

- If you are invited to a house to eat, it is polite to remove your shoes once inside the home of your host. You'll want to wait to be told just where you should sit, and those who are oldest are always served first and begin to eat first. If you can eat with chopsticks, make sure you set them down on the table after so many bites, or if you talk or take a drink. And remember, you should not eat food with your hands. It's not considered polite!

29

LITHUANIAN
A language spoken in
LITHUANIA

COUNTRY FAST FACTS

ESTONIA
RUSSIA
LATVIA
BALTIC SEA
Vilnius ★
RUSSIA
BELARUS
POLAND

Square Miles: 25,212

Population: 2,823,859

Life Expectancy: 75 years

Literacy: 99.8%

Internet Users: 2,122,884

Internet Code: .lt

Money Unit: Litai

SPEAKING LITHUANIAN

Hello: Labas (law bus)
Goodbye: Viso gero (vissa guy roh)
Thank you: Achiu (ah choo)
Peace: Taika (tie caw)

Labas!

That's how I say hello! Just a little under three million people speak Lithuanian in my country. Our capital city is Vilnius, and throughout our country nearly 80 percent of people are Roman Catholic. We also have people who are Russian Orthodox, Protestant, and other religions. Achiu for your wonderful visit! May you have beautiful taika in your life.

Viso gero, friend!!!

We gained our independence from the Soviet Union here in Lithuania in 1991. The medieval Gediminas Tower flew our flag once we were free.

Fear and love do not go together.
Lithuanian Proverb

DID YOU KNOW?

- There are literally thousands of storks that live throughout our country, and the people still share the story of babies being brought by the storks; for fun, of course!

- Believe it or not, bread and salt are considered very important in Lithuanian culture. It is given to important guests and even to newly married couples here. It represents the vital things of life that nurture and flavor it.

- On a traditional Christmas Eve dinner here in Lithuania we serve 12 distinct dishes, often consisting of fish, vegetables, and other such items, and the number represents the 12 Apostles.

- There are many wonderful kinds of food eaten throughout my country. Several traditional dishes are favorites, including borscht (a cold beet soup, with cucumbers and greens), cepelinai (a dumpling dish of meat and potatoes), and vedarai (intestines that are stuffed with potatoes). Delicious!

MANDARIN

A language spoken in

CHINA

COUNTRY FAST FACTS

RUSSIA

KAZAKHSTAN   MONGOLIA

Beijing ★

INDIA

VIETNAM

Square Miles: 3,705,406

Population:
1,379,302,771

Life Expectancy:
76 years

Literacy:
96.4%

Internet Users:
730,723,960

Internet Code:
.cn

Money Unit:
Renminbi Yuan

SPEAKING MANDARIN

Hello: Nǐ hǎo (nee how)
Goodbye: Zàijìan (shay shawn)
Thank you: Xìexìe (shay shay)
Peace: He ping (hee ping)

Nǐ hǎo!

Saying hello from China! There are over 1,379,000,000 people in our country, and most of these speak Mandarin Chinese. Beijing is our capital city. Though our country is officially declared atheist, we do have a large number of people who follow Daoism and Buddhism, and a few that are Christians or Muslims. Xìexìe for stopping by! May you and your family be blessed with he ping.

Zàijìan, friend!!!

These terraces used for raising rice are called the Dragon's Backbone, and were begun around 700 years ago.

DID YOU KNOW?

- They had ice cream here in China thousands of years ago! It was made with snow, some milk, and a little cooked rice.

- There are only around 200 family names in China, though around 20 percent of the people in the world live here! In Chinese, your last name or surname is written first then your first name follows; we do not use middle names.

- Chinese is one of the oldest written languages still being spoken, along with Greek. They both go back around 3,500 years! Chinese characters are delicately painted images from what were once pictures. Now they are symbols that represent thousands of things.

- Many ancient inventions came from China, including the compass, gun powder, and more modern forms of paper, and it just so happens that this book was printed here! Also, tea originated here, and has been around for 2,000 or so years.

VISA

VISA

11

CHINA

HONG KONG

WORLD

(3009)

IMMIGRATION

A book holds a house of gold.
Mandarin Proverb

NORWEGIAN

A language spoken in

NORWAY

COUNTRY FAST FACTS

NORWEGIAN SEA

SWEDEN

FINLAND

Oslo ★

ESTONIA

Square Miles: 125,020

Population:
5,320,045

Life Expectancy:
82 years

Literacy:
100%

Internet Users:
5,122,904

Internet Code:
.no

Money Unit:
Norwegian Kroner

SPEAKING NORWEGIAN

Hello: Goddag (goo dock)
Goodbye: Ha det bra (hah dett brow)
Thank you: Takk (talk)
Peace: Fred (freedt)

Goddag!

That's how I say hello!
Here in Norway almost all of our
5,320,045 people speak Norwegian. Look
for our capital city, Oslo, on the map. Do you
see it in the southern end? Just over 85 percent
of our people are members of the Church of Norway.
There are a small number of people who are Pentecostal,
Roman Catholic, Muslim, and other religions. Takk for
your visit today! Fred to you and those you love.

Ha det bra, friend!!!

34

We have around 1,600 glaciers that cover one percent of our land.

DID YOU KNOW?

- Even though Norway exports more oil than most other countries, our price of gas (also called petrol) is higher than almost anywhere in the world.

- The average person here in Norway drinks more than 15 times as much coffee as those in Ireland.

- If you like frozen pizza, you would fit in perfectly in Norway. One particular type is our favorite, the Grandiosa, of which we eat about 20,000,000 every year! And if you like fish dipped in lye and washed off with water, you will love lutefisk, a traditional Norwegian dish regarded as a delicacy. Speaking of food, one of the best-loved cheeses here just happens to be brown.

- The most famous Norwegian playwright is Henrik Ibsen, known around the world for his play "A Doll's House."

On the road between the homes of friends, grass does not grow.

Norwegian Proverb

35

ORIYA

A language spoken in **INDIA**

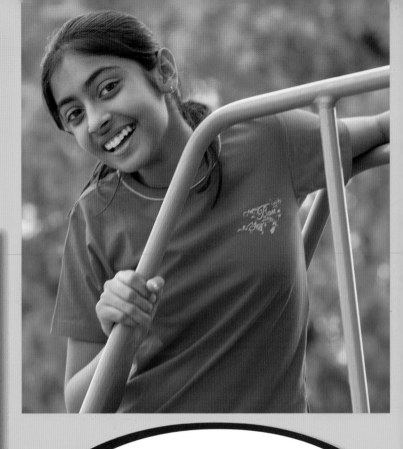

COUNTRY FAST FACTS

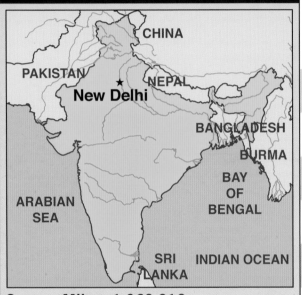

CHINA
PAKISTAN
NEPAL
New Delhi
BANGLADESH
BURMA
BAY OF BENGAL
ARABIAN SEA
SRI LANKA
INDIAN OCEAN

Square Miles: 1,269,219

Population:
1,281,935,911

Life Expectancy:
69 years

Literacy:
71.2%

Internet Users:
374,328,160

Internet Code:
.in

Money Unit:
Indian Rupees

SPEAKING ORIYA

Hello: Namaskar (nah ma scar)
Goodbye: Vidaaya (vid eye ya)
Thank you: Dhanyabahd (dun ya bawd)
Peace: Shanty (shawn tee)

Namaskar!

Saying hello to you! Most of the 31 million speakers of Oriya, my language, live in India here in the state of Orissa. Overall, India has about 1,281,900,000 people! New Delhi is our capital city, and within the country over 80 percent of the people are Hindu. We also have Muslim, Christian, Sikhs, and others. Dhanyabahd for your time today! Be filled with shanti.

Vidaaya, friend!!!

The River Indus, near where some of the first people here made their homes, inspired the name India.

If you live in the river you should make friends with the crocodile.
Oriya Proverb

DID YOU KNOW?

- The people here in India go to the movies around 3,000,000,000 times per year, which is more than any other country.

- Star anise is an eight or twelve pointed star-shaped, dry fruit that is used to cook here in India. It tastes a little like licorice, and might be mixed with curry or in dishes from sweet pies and cookies to veggies and meats.

- There are more universities in India than in any other country. It's interesting that many consider Takshila, an educational institution created here around 700 B.C., to be the world's first university.

- You will find the most post offices in India, more than any other nation, with just over 150,000.

- A lot of wonderful contributions came from here in India, including the number zero, the game of chess, algebra, and trigonometry. Hope you like math!

PASHTO

A language spoken in

AFGHANISTAN

COUNTRY FAST FACTS

UZBEKISTAN • CHINA
TURKMENISTAN • TAJIKISTAN
IRAN
Kabul ★
PAKISTAN • INDIA

Square Miles: 251,827

Population:
34,124,811

Life Expectancy:
51 years

Literacy:
38.2%

Internet Users:
3,531,770

Internet Code:
.af

Money Unit:
Afghanis

SPEAKING PASHTO

Hello: Salam aleikum (saw lahm lie coom)

Goodbye: Da khoday-pe-aman
(dah ko day peh aman)

Thank you: Tashakor (tash ah koor)

Peace: Amniat (ahm nee ott)

Salam aleikum!

This is how I say hello in
Afghanistan! Over one million people
speak my language of Pashto here among
the 34,124,811 population. Of those, around 80
percent are Sunni Muslim, and around 19 percent
are Shia Muslim. See if you can find our capital city of
Kabul. Tashakor for your visit! Be blessed with amniat.

Da khoday-pe-aman, friend!!!

Many of the trucks in our country are covered in exquisite paintings, very detailed and beautiful. The roads look like wondrous moving museums of trucks, brightly detailed with reflective materials that make them very visible and much safer when driving at night.

DID YOU KNOW?

- People here in Afghanistan love sports involving kites. This involves kite fighting and kite running, where kite strings are cut in the air and people run to chase after them.

- One of the most important parts of our meals here in Afghanistan is the bread, specifically naan or nan, which is an unleavened flat bread.

- Pashto or Pashtu is a common language here in Afghanistan, spoken by the Pashtun people. Dari is another language spoken here, and is used by the Tajiks. These names refer to the people or their ethnic groups, which also include the Hazaras, Kyrgyz, Turkmen, and Uzbeks throughout regions of our country.

- Ancient oil lamps were often coated in brass, shaped in very decorative patterns. These are still made today, mostly for ornamental purposes.

VISA

VISA

AFGHANISTAN

Skill is stronger than strength.
Pashto Proverb

QUECHUA
A language spoken in
BOLIVIA

COUNTRY FAST FACTS

Population:	11,138,234
Life Expectancy:	69 years
Literacy:	92.5%
Internet Users:	4,354,678
Internet Code:	.bo
Money Unit:	Bolivianos

Square Miles: 424,164

SPEAKING QUECHUA

Hello: Raphi (raw fee)
Goodbye: Tupananchiskama
(too pan an kiss comma)
Thank you: Yusulpayki (yoo sool pie key)
Peace: Qasikay (kaw see kay)

Raphi!

That's the way I say hello!
There are over two million speakers
of Quechua here in Bolivia, out of the
over 11,000,000 people. About 95 percent
of our people are Roman Catholic, with a small
percentage of Protestants. Come see our capital of La
Paz sometime! Yusulpayki for your friendship!
May all you do be filled with qasikay.

Tupananchiskama, friend!!!

An ancient temple dating back as far as 1,500 years was found deep within Lake Titicaca in 2000. These ancient ruins under the water revealed a detailed roadway, a wall just over 2,500 feet in length, and terraces for growing crops.

DID YOU KNOW?

- There is a huge slab of limestone in Sucre that holds the impression of nearly 5,000 dinosaur footprints. Here one can find the prints of nearly 300 different species of dinosaur at what is considered one of the largest paleontological sites in the world.

- There are three official languages here in Bolivia including Spanish and Quechuan, as well as Aymaran, which existed as a language before the Spanish came to the area.

- The Quechua people are descendents of the Incas, who lived in this area over 500 years ago and built huge palaces and temples. The Incan Empire was once spread over an area some 2,000 miles long. The Inca people used llamas for carrying heavy loads and fibers for cloth, and the Quechua people still have llamas today.

- The yerba mate plant is made into a drink much like tea, simmered and sipped from a gourd with a bombilla, a metal straw.

SERVICIO NACIONAL DE MIGRACION
REPUBLICA DE BOLIVIA

022ZSA
Admitido Hasta:

VISA

Do not steal, do not lie, don't be lazy.
Quechua Proverb

RUSSIAN
A language spoken in
RUSSIA

COUNTRY FAST FACTS

Population:
142,257,519

Life Expectancy:
71 years

Literacy:
99.7%

Internet Users:
108,772,470

Internet Code:
.ru

Square Miles: 6,601,668

Money Unit:
Russian rubles

SPEAKING RUSSIAN

Hello: Zdravstvujte (strawst voo chaw)
Goodbye: Dos vidanija (duss vee dun yaw)
Thank you: Spasibo (spy see bow)
Peace: Mir (meer)

Zdravstvujte!

Saying hello from Russia! We
have over 142,000,000 people, and
our country is divided into 11 time zones!
The majority of the people here speak Russian,
and there are Russian Orthodox Christians,
Muslims, and other Christian denominations, too.
You can see our capital of Moscow on the far western
side of our nation. Spasibo for coming to my land!
Be filled with mir today.

Dos vidanija, friend!!!

Russia is the largest country in the world. It is so big that a train ride across our country takes around a full week, and a plane trip takes about ten hours, from one side to the other.

ENTERED ON:
Moscow | Gorod Moskva | Russia
VISA APPROVED

We do not care of what we have, but we cry when it is lost.
Russian Proverb

DID YOU KNOW?

- The borders of Russia and the United States are only two miles apart in some parts of Alaska.

- We truly like to celebrate life and love, and so we often place great significance on birthdays and anniversaries of friends and family. We love to throw big parties for those we love. Russian nesting dolls have been wonderful gifts here since 1890.

- Because of the long, cold winters here in Russia, we have come to use a lot of cured, salted, and smoked chicken, fish, and beef that will preserve well through the winter months. We also eat a lot of pickled and salted vegetables, as well as many types of delicious breads.

- It has long been a Russian custom to share tea and honey cakes. Often honey cakes are given as gifts at Christmas and Easter. You might find them in the shape of horses, deer, dolls, birds, and even cradles when given to a newly married couple.

SPANISH

A language spoken in

MEXICO

COUNTRY FAST FACTS

UNITED STATES

GULF OF MEXICO

Mexico City ★

NORTH PACIFIC OCEAN

BELIZE

GUATEMALA
EL SALVADOR

Square Miles: 758,449

Population:
124,574,795

Life Expectancy:
76 years

Literacy:
94.5%

Internet Users:
73,334,032

Internet Code:
.mx

Money Unit:
Mexican Pesos

SPEAKING SPANISH

Hello: Hola (oh law)
Goodbye: Adiós (aw dee oss)
Thank you: Gracias (graw see us)
Peace: Paz (pas)

Hola!

This is how I say hello! Here in Mexico, with Mexico City as our capital, over 115,000,000 people speak Spanish; nearly all the population. Over 75 percent of the population is Roman Catholic, while there are some Protestants as well. Gracias for your time! Hope you have paz filling your home.

Adiós, friend!!!

Mexico is the historic homeland of the ancient Aztec Empire, dating back to the 1300s. Mexico City, one of the largest cities in the world, resides upon the ancient Aztec city of Tenochtitlan, which was destroyed by the Spanish armies.

DID YOU KNOW?

- Children in most cultures have what is called a surname or last name. This is often the family name of the father, and passes from generation to generation. Here in Mexico, children take the surname of both their mother and their father.

- Of the over 330,000,000 Spanish-speaking people worldwide, you will find the greatest population of Spanish speakers here in Mexico.

- Music and dance are richly woven into our culture, rooted in the vibrant history of the arts throughout Mexico.

- Next to the border between the United States and Canada, the border between the United States and Mexico is the largest, covering almost 2,000 miles of land.

- Corn is vital to the people here in Mexico, grown on about half of the existing farmland. We use it in nearly all our meals, as it is found in burritos, salads, tortillas, and more.

VISA **13** VISA

VISA

MEXICO

IMMIGRATION OFFICER ADF023

A wise man changes his mind, a fool never.
Spanish Proverb

45

TURKISH

A language spoken in

TURKEY

COUNTRY FAST FACTS

RUSSIA
ROMANIA
GEORGIA
BULGARIA
BLACK SEA
ARMENIA
★ Ankara
SYRIA
IRAQ
MEDITERRANEAN SEA

Square Miles: 302,534

Population:	80,845,215
Life Expectancy:	75 years
Literacy:	95.6%
Internet Users:	46,838,412
Internet Code:	.tr
Money Unit:	Turkish liras

SPEAKING TURKISH

Hello: Merhaba (mare haw baw)

Goodbye: gule gule (goo lay goo law)

Thank you: Tesekkur ederim (te shay koor eh dur um)

Peace: Sulh (sool)

Merhaba!

Saying hello from Turkey! Of the 80,845,215 people, most of us here speak Turkish and 99 percent of the people are Muslims; a very small percentage are Christians. See if you can find our capital city of Ankara on the map. Tesekkur ederim for coming so far! Be filled with sulh.

Gule gule, friend!!!

Early Christians lived in the odd rock formations found in the area of Cappadocia. Formed from volcanic eruptions, they carved out homes and churches in the soft stone, providing shelter and protection.

DID YOU KNOW?

- The most famous city in the world that is on two continents (Europe and Asia) is Istanbul, located here in Turkey.

- If someone was caught drinking coffee in 16th or 17th century Turkey he or she would be put to death. Now coffee houses, called kahve, are found in nearly every village and town. These are wondrous gathering places to socialize with friends and family. Try the Turkish tea, because the coffee here is very strong.

- Our foods have been influenced by many cultures, though there are some traditional items found in most meals. Grilled or roasted meats, rice, and vegetables are often eaten, flavored with cumin, dill, garlic, and other spices. Aubergine (eggplant) and lamb are two very common foods in most homes here. For dessert, halva is often enjoyed, which is like a sweet cake made with sesame seeds.

No road is long with good company.
Turkish Proverb

47

UKRAINIAN

A language spoken in

UKRAINE

COUNTRY FAST FACTS

BELARUS
RUSSIA
Kyiv ★
POL
MOLDOVA
ROMANIA
BLACK SEA

Square Miles: 233,031

Population:
44,033,874

Life Expectancy:
72 years

Literacy:
99.8%

Internet Users:
23,202,067

Internet Code:
.ua

Money Unit:
Hryvnia

SPEAKING UKRAINIAN

Hello: Vitayu (vee tie you)
Goodbye: Do pobachennya
(doe poe baa chen yah)
Thank you: Dyakuju (jah coo joo)
Peace: Mir (mirror)

Vitayu!

This is how I say hello! Most of our 44,033,874 people here speak Ukrainian, and about half of those are Ukrainian Orthodox. There are also Ukrainian Greek Catholics, Roman Catholics, Protestants, Jewish, and others. Look close on the map and you will see Kyiv, our capital city. Dyakuju for your visiting! Let mir fill your heart.

Do pobachennya, friend!!!

Ukraine was once a part of the Soviet Union. On August 24th, 1991, we celebrated our independence.

DID YOU KNOW?

- On top of Boim's chapel is a statue of Christ sitting on the Cross, the only one of its kind in the world.

- Bread is produced here in large quantities, giving our land the nickname "the bread basket of Europe."

- The pysanka is a beautifully ornamented Ukrainian Easter egg. The name means "to write" because the decorations are actually written with beeswax.

- The people here are considered quite kind and friendly. When we gather together we always have food, offering those who are visitors something to eat as well as something to drink. It is considered quite rude not to offer something to someone if you are eating something yourself.

- If you are invited to join a group of people, know that they often greet with a strong handshake, creating a warm environment. If invited over to someone's home, it is polite to bring a small gift of cake or flowers. Remember never to begin eating until your host invites you to begin.

Only when you have eaten a lemon do you appreciate what sugar is.
Ukrainian Proverb

VIETNAMESE
A language spoken in
VIETNAM

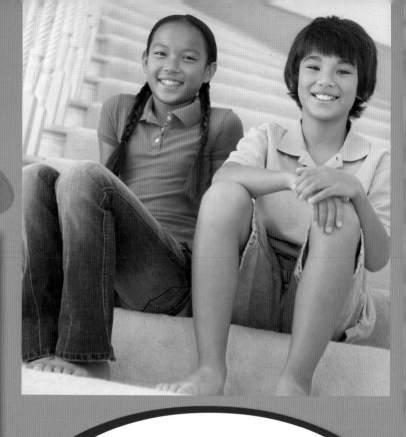

COUNTRY FAST FACTS

Map showing CHINA, Hanoi, LAOS, THAILAND, KAMPUCHEA, SOUTH CHINA SEA

Square Miles: 127,880

Population:
96,160,163

Life Expectancy:
73 years

Literacy:
94.5%

Internet Users:
49,741,000

Internet Code:
.vn

Money Unit:
Dong

SPEAKING VIETNAMESE

Hello: Chao anh (chow awn - to a man)
chao chi (chow chee - to a woman)
Goodbye: Tam biêt (tem bee et)
Thank you: Cám ón (cam on)
Peace: Hoa bình (how bin)

Chao anh, if you're a guy, or chao chi, if you're a girl!

Saying hello from Vietnam! Of the 96,160,163 people in my country, most of us speak Vietnamese. In our capital city of Hanoi you can find Buddhists, Catholics, Hoa Hao, Cao Dai, Protestants, and Muslims, though most people here do not have a religion. Cám ón for coming to Vietnam! May you and your family be filled with hoa bình.

Tam biêt, friend!!!

There are beautiful blue boats that sail in the bay off the coastal city of Nha Trang. The bay is considered one of the most stunning in the world.

DID YOU KNOW?

- There are no coins used in Vietnam, only paper money.

- China ruled the people of Vietnam for hundreds of years. We gained our freedom in A.D. 938 when our army defeated an armada of Chinese military ships. Along with rice, we also eat beef, chicken, fish, and pork with our meals, often dipped in fish or soy sauces.

- Food differs slightly depending on where you are in Vietnam. In the north, you'll find many stir fried meals, though less meat, and saltier dishes. In the south, we often add sweetness to our food with sugar or coconut milk, and spicy tastes with chili peppers. Central Vietnamese meals will consist of spicier dishes with lots of colorful foods and slightly smaller portions.

- It was French missionaries here who planted the first coffee in 1857. Vietnam exports more coffee than any nation other than Brazil, mostly going to the United States.

VISA

VIETNAM - IMMIGRATION

NỘI BÀI

211A

WORLD

A day of traveling will bring a basketful of learning.

Vietnamese Proverb

51

WELSH

A language spoken in the

UNITED KINGDOM

COUNTRY FAST FACTS

IRELAND

London ★

FRANCE

Square Miles: 94,058

Population:	64,769,452
Life Expectancy:	81 years
Literacy:	99%
Internet Users:	61,064,454
Internet Code:	.uk
Money Unit:	British Pounds

SPEAKING WELSH

Hello: Shwmae (s my or shoo my)
Goodbye: Hwyl fawr (well far)
Thank you: Diolch (dee olich)
Peace: Heddwich (head vig)

Shwmae!

Just saying hello! Wales is a part of Great Britain. Over 560,000 people here can speak Welsh. Our capital, though, is in London, England. Throughout Great Britain you will find over 64,000,000 people — 71 percent are Christians, with a smaller amount of Muslims, Hindus, and other religions. Diolch for your wonderful visit! Find your life full of heddwich today.

Hwyl fawr!

The Jurassic Coast of Dorset, England, is considered a World Heritage Coastline, and is filled with easy-to-find fossils from Noah's flood. Try to collect only the loose ones, so as to preserve the beauty of the region for years to come. To be safe, avoid the cliff areas and just search on the beaches. Mary Anning, a famous fossil hunter, lost her dog when part of a cliff face crashed down upon him while they were out.

DID YOU KNOW?

- Welsh Rabbit, or Welsh rarebit, is a popular food here that is made up of a piece of toast covered in melted cheese with spices.

- We drink more tea on average than any person of any other country in the world.

- Windsor Castle happens to be the oldest royal home in the world that is still lived in by the royal family!

- Lots of people from around the world have come to live here in the United Kingdom. Nearly one quarter of the population in London was born outside England.

- The symbol on the traditional Welsh flag happens to be a red dragon, specifically the Welsh Dragon or Draig Goch, and has been depicted on the back of the British one pound coin.

VISA

A nation without a language is a nation without a heart.
Welsh Proverb

XHOSA

A language spoken in **SOUTH AFRICA**

COUNTRY FAST FACTS

ZIMBABWE

NAMIBIA

BOTSWANA

MOZAMBIQUE

Pretoria ★

SWAZILAND

Bloemfontein ★

LESOTHO

SOUTH AFRICA

★ Cape Town

Square Miles: 470,693

Population:	54,841,552
Life Expectancy:	63 years
Literacy:	95.4%
Internet Users:	29,322,380
Internet Code:	.za
Money Unit:	Rand

SPEAKING XHOSA

Hello: Molo (mow low)

Goodbye: Sala kakuhle (saw law kah coo lay)

Thank you: Enkosi (in co see)

Peace: Uxolo (xow low)

Molo!

This is how I say hello in Xhosa! You say the word like this: co suh. Just a little over 7,000,000 people say hello like that here in South Africa, though over 54,000,000 people live here. We actually have three capitals. Pretoria is our administrative capital, Cape Town is our legislative capital, and Bloemfontein is our judicial capital. There are many Christians here, as well as Muslims and others. Enkosi for your treasured time! Uxolo to you.

Sala kakuhle, friend!!!

Nearly half of the world's gold comes from South Africa.

DID YOU KNOW?

- The oldest city here in South Africa is Cape Town, which was the first European settlement, established in 1652.

- There are many national parks here, but Kruger National Park is one of the most popular. Considered one of the most beautiful in the world, it is the perfect environment for African wild dogs, elephants, giraffes, hyenas, lions, monkeys, and rhinoceros.

- Many of us eat three meals each day. A breakfast is often hot cereal made of cornmeal porridge, called putupap, with either coffee or tea to drink.

- There are many restaurants here in South Africa, those that serve traditional foods as well as those from international chains. Many of us do enjoy going out to eat, and enjoy many diverse cultural foods like Chinese, Japanese, Moroccan, and West African, with interesting meal choices like ostrich meat and umvubo, which is made with sour milk and dried pap (porridge).

PASSPORT CONTROL
DEPARTURE

CAPE TOWN
SOUTH AFRICA

VISA

Throats are all alike in swallowing.
Xhosa Proverb

YORUBA
A language spoken in NIGERIA

COUNTRY FAST FACTS

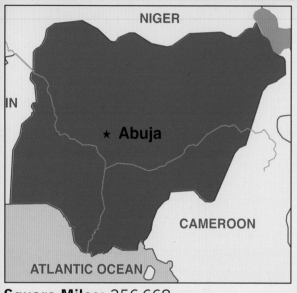

NIGER

★ Abuja

CAMEROON

ATLANTIC OCEAN

Square Miles: 356,668

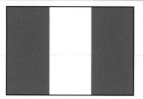

Population:
190,632,261

Life Expectancy:
53 years

Literacy:
59.6%

Internet Users:
47,759,904

Internet Code:
.ng

Money Unit:
Nairas

SPEAKING YORUBA

Hello: E kú àárò (ee coo ah row)
Goodbye: O dàbo (oh daw bow)
Thank you: E se (ee see)
Peace: Alaafia (all ah fee ah)

E kú àárò!

Wishing you hello! Over 20 million speak my language in Nigeria, out of a population of just over 190,000,000 people. In the center of our country you can see our capital city of Abuja. Half of our people are Muslims, another 40 percent are Christians, and of those remaining many have tribal beliefs they hold. E se for coming to see me! Be filled with alaafia.

O dàbo, friend!!!

56

A single massive stone is called a monolith. We have one called Zuma Rock that is not far from our capital.

A proverb is the horse that can carry one swiftly to the discovery of ideas.
Yoruba Proverb

DID YOU KNOW?

- The kids here love soccer. Also, a board game called Ayo is often played. It takes two players that use a board of 12 cups and seeds.

- One of the favorite foods here is the plantain. It's related to the banana family, and is usually either fried, stewed, or toasted.

- It is regarded as an insult to give something to someone older than you if it is in your left hand.

- The rhythmic music of Nigeria is known around the world. Much music of the Yoruba people involves intricate drumming patterns.

- It's very warm here in Nigeria. In fact, the average temperature is 90 degrees year round. There are more people in this country than any other African nation. In fact, about one-fifth of all people in Africa live in Nigeria.

- Hospitality is very important to the people here, caring deeply for our guests. It can even be considered rude to say "thank you" when offered food, since it is expected of a host to provide for their guests.

ZULU

A language spoken in

SWAZILAND

COUNTRY FAST FACTS

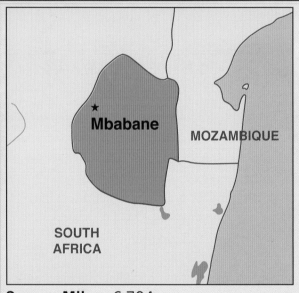

★ Mbabane

MOZAMBIQUE

SOUTH AFRICA

Square Miles: 6,704

Population:
1,467,152

Life Expectancy:
52 years

Literacy:
87.5%

Internet Users:
414,724

Internet Code:
.sz

Money Unit:
Emalangeni

SPEAKING ZULU

Hello: Sawubona (sow oo bow nah)
Goodbye: Hamba hahle (ham baw haw lay)
Thank you: Ngiyabona (gee aw bone ah)
Peace: Ukuthula (oo coo tho law)

Sawubona!

Greeting you with my hello!
you find Mbabane, our capital c
few people here speak Zulu, though
to South Africa with over nine million s
are Zionist Christians here, as well as R
Muslims, and others all living near th
Ngiyabona for your travels here! Take u

Hamba hahle, friend!!!

Here in Swaziland, if you are from the Nguni people, you build your huts in the shape of a beehive. If you are from the Sotho people, you build your hut with windows and complete doorways.

Follow the customs or flee the country.
Zulu Proverb

DID YOU KNOW?

- Zulu warriors of the southern regions of Africa were once considered a fierce people because of their skills in fighting. Many of the Zulu people now live in the larger cities and work alongside all our other citizens.

- The people here eat a variety of foods, some common Western type foods like avocado, beans, and pumpkin, as well as traditional foods like antelope and other "wild meats," as they are called.

- The name of our country comes from a former king, King Mswati. We call the country eSwatini.

- Rock paintings found here date back thousands of years, and this rich culture of art continues to this day, found in the exquisite and colorful masks and other works of artistry.

- Our first Zulu book of grammar actually came out in Norway in 1850, and was written by Hans Schreuder, a Norwegian missionary. In 1883, the first Zulu document came out; it was a translation of the Bible.

COUNTRY FACTS AT A GLANCE

Country	Population	Rank	Life Expectancy	Rank	Literacy	Rank
Afghanistan	34,124,811	17	51 years	14	38.2%	15
Armenia	3,045,191	23	75 years	7	99.7%	3
Australia	23,232,413	18	82 years	3	99.0%	4
Bangladesh	157,826,578	5	73 years	8	72.8%	13
Bolivia	11,138,234	20	69 years	11	92.5%	11
Canada	35,623,680	16	82 years	3	99.0%	4
China	1,379,302,771	1	76 years	6	96.4%	7
Germany	80,594,017	11	81 years	4	99.0%	4
Iceland	339,747	26	83 years	2	99.0%	4
India	1,281,935,911	2	69 years	11	71.2%	14
Israel	8,299,706	21	82 years	3	97.8%	6
Japan	126,451,398	7	85 years	1	99.0%	4
Lithuania	2,823,859	24	75 years	7	99.8%	2
Mexico	124,574,795	8	76 years	6	94.5%	10
Netherlands	17,084,719	19	81 years	4	99.0%	4
Nigeria	190,632,261	4	53 years	13	59.6%	14
Norway	5,320,045	22	82 years	3	100.0%	1
Russia	142,257,519	6	71 years	10	99.7%	3
South Africa	54,841,552	13	63 years	12	95.4%	9
South Korea	51,181,299	14	82 years	3	97.9%	5
Swaziland	1,467,152	25	52 years	13	87.5%	12
Turkey	80,845,215	10	75 years	7	95.6%	8
Ukraine	44,033,874	15	72 years	9	99.8%	2
United Kingdom	64,769,452	12	81 years	4	99.0%	4
United States	326,625,791	3	80 years	5	99.0%	4
Vietnam	96,160,163	9	73 years	8	94.5%	10

Country Facts at a Glance compares only the 26 countries in this book.

Country	Square Miles	Rank	Internet Users	Rank	Money Unit
Afghanistan	251,827	12	3,531,770	22	Afghanis
Armenia	11,483	24	1,891,775	24	Drams
Australia	2,988,901	5	20,288,409	17	Australian Dollars
Bangladesh	55,597	19	28,499,324	15	Taka
Bolivia	424,164	9	4,354,678	21	Bolivianos
Canada	3,855,102	2	31,770,034	13	Canadian Dollar
China	3,705,406	4	730,723,960	1	Renminbi Yuan
Germany	137,846	15	72,365,643	7	Euros
Iceland	39,768	20	329,967	26	Icelandic Kronur
India	1,269,219	6	374,328,160	2	Indian Rupees
Israel	8,019	25	6,521,539	19	New Israeli Shekels
Japan	145,913	14	116,565,962	4	Yen
Lithuania	25,212	22	2,122,884	23	Litai
Mexico	758,449	7	73,334,032	6	Mexican Pesos
Netherlands	16,039	23	15,385,203	18	Euros
Nigeria	356,668	10	47,759,904	10	Nairas
Norway	125,020	17	5,122,904	20	Norwegian Kronur
Russia	6,601,668	1	108,772,470	5	Russian Rubles
South Africa	470,693	8	29,322,380	14	Rand
South Korea	38,502	21	44,153,000	12	South Korean Won
Swaziland	6,704	26	414,724	25	Emalangeni
Turkey	302,534	11	46,838,412	11	Turkish Liras
Ukraine	233,031	13	23,202,067	16	Hryvnia
United Kingdom	94,058	18	61,064,454	8	British Pounds
United States	3,794,100	3	246,809,221	3	Dollar
Vietnam	127,880	16	49,741,000	9	Dong

NAME THAT FLAG

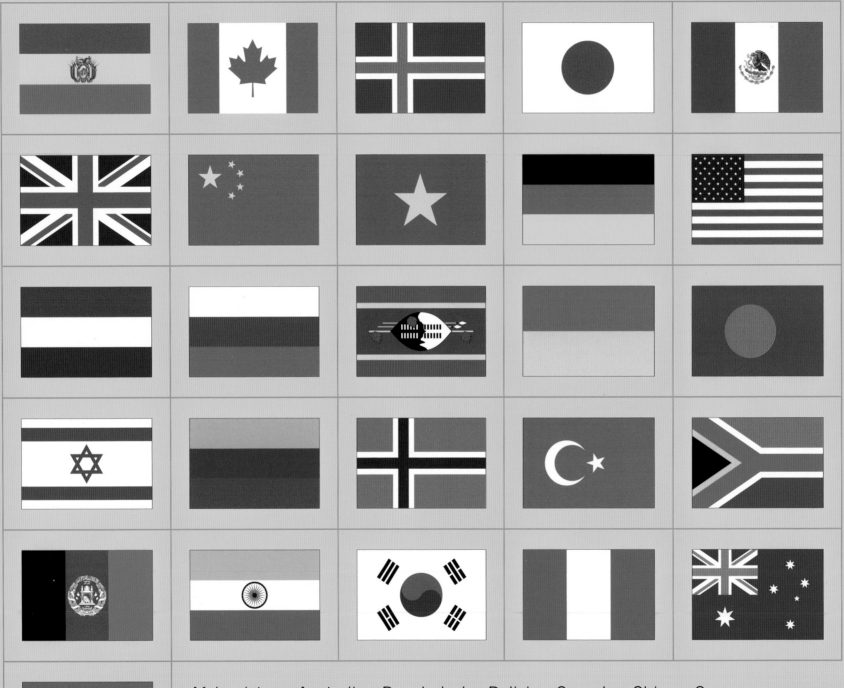

Afghanistan • Australia • Bangladesh • Bolivia • Canada • China • Germany
Iceland • India • Israel • Japan • Lithuania • Mexico • The Netherlands • Nigeria
Norway • Russia • South Africa • South Korea • Swaziland • Turkey • Ukraine
United Kingdom • United States of America • Vietnam

NAME THAT COUNTRY

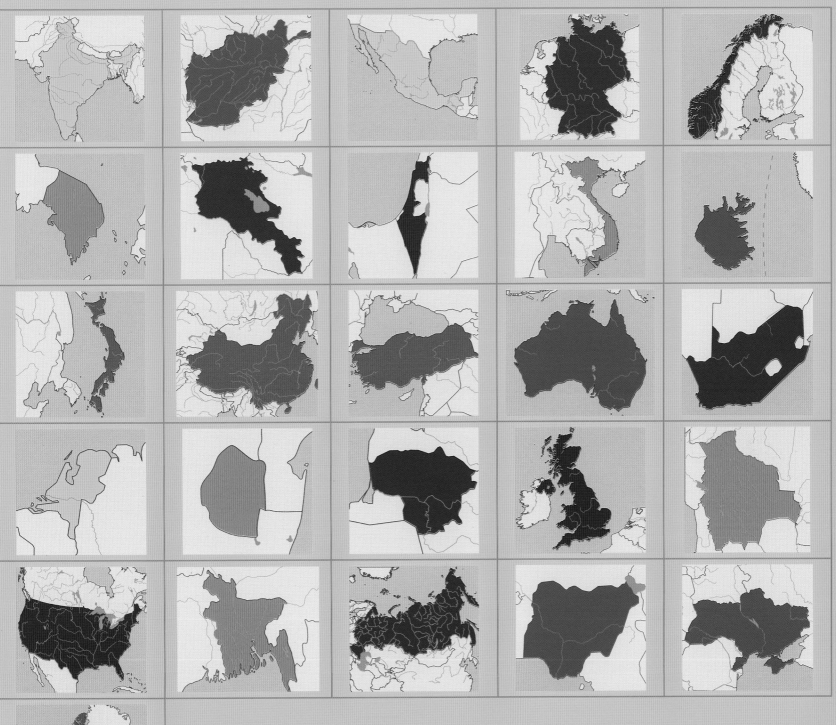

Here's a challenge for you. See if you can name all the countries by their shape. Already can do that? Then how about guessing all the capital cities, neighboring countries, and perhaps even their continents! Consider photocopying the page and cutting up the images for flash cards too. Have fun!

BREAKING THE LANGUAGE BARRIER

So many things can prevent us from helping others, and language differences are just one of those. Here are ten ways you can help children around the world, even if you can't speak their language. Realize that some children struggle each day just to find something to eat. You might already be doing something right now in your own neighborhood or you may want to begin something special. The Bible states that *"Religion that God our Father accepts as pure and faultless is this: to look after orphans and widows in their distress and to keep one self from being polluted by the world"* (James 1:27).

 AIDS Care Fund
www.aidscarefund.org

We provide counseling, support groups, literature, a toll-free hotline, and Christian homes for children dying of AIDS.

 Children's Hope Chest
www.hopechest.org

Children's Hope Chest believes that every orphan has the right to know God, experience the blessing of family, and have the opportunity to develop independent living skills.

 Compassion International
www.compassion.com

Compassion International exists as a Christian child advocacy ministry that releases children from spiritual, economic, social, and physical poverty and enables them to become responsible, fulfilled Christian adults.

 Kids Around the World
www.kidsaroundtheworld.com

Kids Around the World is a faith-based organization that builds playgrounds to bring joy and hope to many children around the world whose lives have been devastated by war, natural disasters, and economic stress.

 Warm Blankets Orphan Care International
www.kinshipunited.org

We unite people separated by war and tragedy, rebuild loving families for orphans and widows, and create networks of local churches and rescue centers.

The Water Project
www.thewaterproject.org

The Water Project, Inc. is a non-profit, charitable organization that works to bring relief to people in communities around the world who suffer needlessly from a lack of access to clean water.

World Vision, Inc.
www.worldvision.org

World Vision is a Christian humanitarian organization dedicated to working with children, families, and their communities worldwide to reach their full potential by tackling the causes of poverty and injustice.

ARRIVAL
ARMENIA

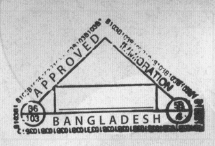
APPROVED
BANGLADESH

USA   IMMIGRATION OFFICER 6079

NETHERLANDS REPUBLIC
ACCEPTED

IMMIGRATION
ARRIVED
SYDNEY AIRPORT
4251
AUSTRALIA

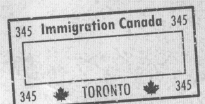
345 Immigration Canada 345
345   TORONTO   345

CHECKPOINT CHARLIE
BERLIN
ARRIVAL
GERMANY

ISRAEL
IMMIGRATION OFFICER
Customs - Jerusalem

1015 IMMIGRATION OFFICER 1015
Landed Until _____
EMPLOYMENT NOT PERMITTED
ICELAND

JAPANIMMIGRATION
上 陸 許 可
入国審査官・日本国
Status : Temporary Visitor
Duration : 9 days
JAPAN IMMIGRATION

REPUBLIC OF KOREA
IMMIGRATION
ARRIVAL
INCHEON AIRPORT 106

IMMIGRATION OFFICER
LITHUANIAN

CHINA
HONG KONG
(30日)
IMMIGRATION

NORWAY - OSLO
DEPARTED FEB

IMMIGRATION
8
5
3
INDIA
NEW DELHI

AFGHANISTAN

SERVICIO NACIONAL DE MIGRACION
REPUBLICA DE BOLIVIA
022ZSA
Admitido Hasta:
30 DIAS

ENTERED ON:
Moscow | Gorod Moskva | Russia
VISA APPOVED

IMMIGRATION OFFICER
MEXICO
ADF023

IMMIGRATION OFFICER
Customs - ANKARA
TURKEY

УКРАЇНА
U K R A I N E
0   0
6   6
3   3
Шегині   460800

VIETNAM - IMMIGRATION
211A

IMMIGRATION - CUSTOMS - LONDON - UK - DEPARTURE

PASSPORT CONTROL
DEPARTURE
CAPE TOWN
SOUTH AFRICA

Nigeria CUSTOMS
IMMIGRATION OFFICER 6079
EMPLOYMENT NOT PERMITTED

IMMIGRATION CONTROL
DEPARTURE
SWAZILAND

You may fill in the date of your visit on the line provided on the stamp.

Please note that these stamps are only representative of official passport stamps.